Seashore Creatures

of the Pacific Northwest

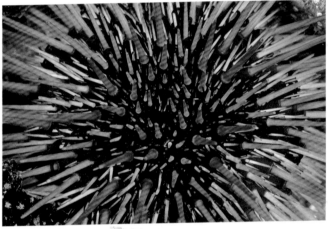

Red sea urchin

J. Duane Sept

Calypso Publishing

All photographs by J. Duane Sept except for the photograph of the author by Susan Servos-Sept (p. 95).

Front cover photos: Olympic National Park, Washington, Giant Green Anemone, Red Rock Crab and Lion's Mane Jelly.
Back cover photo: Leather Star.

To view addional images by Duane Sept visit: www.septphoto.com

Printed and bound in China.

Calypso Publishing
P. O. Box 1141
Sechelt, BC Canada
VON 3A0
www.calypso-publishing.com

Library and Archives Canada Cataloguing in Publication

Sept, J. Duane, 1950-
 Common seashore creatures of the Pacific northwest / Duane Sept.

Includes index.
ISBN 978-0-9739819-2-6

 1. Seashore animals--Northwest, Pacific--Identification. I. Title.
QH104.5.N6S463 2008   591.769′909795   C2008-900791-3

Table of Contents

Quick Photo Guide to the Seashore Creatures

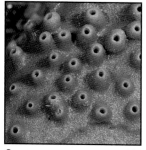
Sponges p. 12

Sea Anemones p. 14

Hydroids p. 18

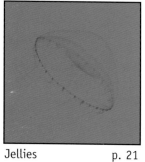
Jellies p. 21

True Jellies p. 22

Marine Worms p. 24

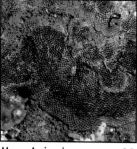
Moss Animals p. 26

Chitons p. 28

Limpets p. 30

Snails p. 34   Nudibranchs p. 42   Bivalves p. 46

Barnacles   p. 60   Isopods   p. 62   Amphipods   p. 64

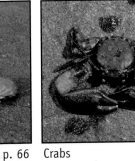

Shrimps   p. 66   Crabs   p. 68   Sea Stars   p. 74

Brittle Stars   p. 78   Sea Urchins   p. 80   Sand Dollar   p. 80

Sea Cucumbers   p. 82   Tunicates   p. 84   Fishes   p. 88

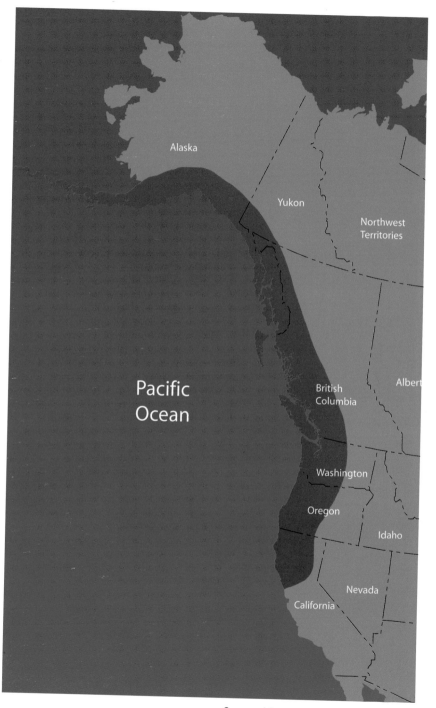

Alaska

Yukon

Northwest
Territories

Pacific
Ocean

British
Columbia

Albert

Washington

Oregon

Idaho

Nevada

California

Geographic area covered in this guide.

Welcome to the Seashore

The Pacific Northwest is well known for its diverse intertidal marine life. Thanks to a combination of wave exposure, shoreline type and plentiful food, a rich abundance of animal and plant life can be found along the narrow strip of land known as the intertidal zone—the area that lies between the highest and lowest tide lines. Intertidal sites are best viewed when the tide reaches their lower levels.

Tides

Tides are caused by the gravitational effects of the moon and sun acting upon the world's oceans. The moon's influence is the stronger one because of its proximity to earth. High tides occur when the moon is closest to the ocean, and the water level rises in response to the gravitational pull of the moon. When both the sun and moon are in the same orientation toward earth, the gravitational pull is greatest on the nearest oceans. When a low tide occurs at one side of earth, the opposite side experiences a high tide to compensate for the change in water level.

Intertidal Habitats

Several types of seashore may be found along our beaches. Each of these habitats is home to species whose physical features are specialized for that environment. Some species may be found in more than one type of habitat.

ROCKY SHORES

A wide variety of creatures can be found on rocky beaches, including various anemones, limpets, chitons and tunicates.

Our shorelines have several intertidal zones, each inhabitated by a particular combination of creatures and plant life. These zones are (from top to bottom) the spray zone, high intertidal zone, middle intertidal zone and low intertidal zone. Some creatures may be found in more than one zone. These zones are present in all intertidal areas, but they are most evident on rocky shorelines.

SANDY SHORES

Marine life forms that are found on sandy beaches include the Pacific razor-clam (p. 56), purple olive (p. 40), and pile worm (p. 25).

MUD SHORES

Creatures found on muddy beaches include the softshell-clam (p. 56) and blue mud shrimp (p. 67).

Intertidal Etiquette

The marine life forms that inhabit our shores are fragile, so please ensure your visit is a positive one for the creatures you have come to enjoy. Be careful where you step, and carefully replace any rocks that you turn over. Creatures that require a moist or wet environment can dry out quickly when exposed to sunlight. When you leave, take care to pack out everything you brought with you. This will make the seashore environment a positive place for other visitors as well as for the marine residents.

Harvesting Shellfish

One of the many ways to enjoy the seashore is to harvest shellfish. If you plan to do so, ensure that you have the necessary licence and check for local restrictions and limits. Local areas are sometimes closed to harvesting because of pollution or algal blooms such as red tide.

PSP (Red Tide) Hotlines

Beach Water Quality Monitoring System (United States)
Web site: http://www.earth911.org/waterquality/index.asp?cluster=0

Alaska 1-800-731-1312
Web site: http://www.dec.state.ak.us/eh/fss/seafood/psphome.htm

British Columbia 1-866-431-3474
Web site: http://www.pac.dfo-mpo.gc.ca/recfish/PSP&contamination_e.htm

Washington 1-800-562-5632
Web site: http://ww4.doh.wa.gov/gis/mogifs/biotoxin.htm

Oregon 1-800-448-2474
Web site: http://oregon.gov/ODA/FSD/shellfish_status.shtml

California 1-800-553-4133
Web site: http://www.cdph.ca.gov/healthinfo/environhealth/water/Pages/
Shellfish.aspx

How to Use This Guide

PHYLUM
This classification comprises a very large group of living organisms, which are often divided further into many classes. For example, both humans and fish belongs to the phylum Chordata, because both species have vertebrae; and both snails and clams belong to the phylum Mollusca because they share one or more internal or external shells, a muscular "foot" and an unsegmented body with a mantle or fold in the body wall.

Class or Family
The class or family is a grouping of one or more genera (see Species Names below) with similar overall characteristics. All oysters, for instance, belong to the oyster family (Ostreidae), which includes several genera.

General Notes
A brief summary of the key identifying features of a class or family of creatures.

Did You Know?
These interesting facts include little-known information on natural history, noteworthy research findings or the habits of a particular creature.

Diet
This section notes the food that a particular group of marine life feed on.

Enemies
The predators that are known to feed upon this family or class are included here.

Reproduction

A brief explanation of the species' propagation and life cycle is summarized in this section.

Habitat

Habitat is the type of area (surface, wave conditions, etc.) in which a species normally lives. Many common species are found in more than one habitat.

Key Features

This section focuses on the characteristics of a species that make it unique. For best results in identifying a species, use the photograph along with the Key Features.

Species Names

A common and a scientific name are listed for each species. Every living organism has a unique scientific name consisting of two parts: the genus or genera (a grouping of species with common characteristics) and the species. Occasionally names change as new scientific information is discovered. The most current or appropriate name is included in this book.

Common names are those used in everyday conversation by people who live in an area where the species occur, so many organisms have several common names.

The Creatures

SPONGES

PHYLUM Porifera

Sponges are primitive life forms that develop in loose aggregations with different types of cells. Water enters the organism through tiny pores called ostia and leaves via larger pores, or oscula. Whip-like flagellae beat the water to help it flow through the sponge. Food enters through the pores as well, and both water and food circulate through the organism in a system of canals. The internal skeleton of most sponges is made up of spicules (rod-shaped structures) inside the tissue of most sponges. There are about 5,000 known species in the world, most of which are found in salt water.

Purple encrusting sponge

Did you know?
Some sponges that live in subtropical parts of the world are very toxic and may cause painful skin blisters if touched.

Diet
Sponges are filter-feeders that capture a variety of food, including detritus particles, plankton and bacteria, by ingesting water.

Enemies
Nudibranchs, snails, chitons and sea stars are known to be predators of some sponges.

Reproduction
Sponges reproduce asexually by budding, or when a small fragment simply breaks away from the parent. Some species also reproduce sexually, since most individuals are hermaphroditic—female one season and male the next.

Habitat
Rocks or rocky shores are the main habitats for most species.

Bread Crumb Sponge
Halichondria panicea
Key Features
Normally green or yellowish, and often encrusts rocks.

Purple Encrusting Sponge
Haliclona permollis
Key Features
Purplish in color, and normally encrusts rocks.

Red Encrusting Sponge
Ophlitaspongia pennata
Key Features
Bright red, and normally en-crusts rocks.

13

SEA ANEMONES, JELLIES & ALLIES

PHYLUM Cnidaria

All members of the phylum Cnidaria (pronounced "Nye-DARE-ee-uh") possess nematocysts (stinging capsules) located on tentacles that circle a single opening. *Cnidos* is a Greek word that means stinging nettles. The phylum includes three classes of animals: Hydrozoa (hydroids), Anthozoa (corals, sea anemones) and scyphozoa (jellies). Most members of this phylum have two basic body forms: medusa and polyp. Many (but not all) individuals transform from one form to another during their life. The polyp is the asexual stage, often attached to a substrate, while the medusa is normally free-swimming. In some species, either the polyp or the medusa stage may be completely absent or reduced.

Anemones, hydroids and jellies are sac-like organisms. They have a central digestive system with a single opening that acts as both mouth and anus. This opening is radial and symmetrical, ringed by tentacles containing stinging capsules. Each stinging capsule is armed with a harpoon-like structure, and some capsules can harm people.

Sea Anemones (Class Anthozoa)

Aggregating anemones

General Notes

Sea anemones live only as polyps and do not have a medusa stage. Sea anemones are able to move from location to another—but very slowly.

Did You Know?

Some species of sea anemones are armed with ascodia, specialized threads with large numbers of nematocysts, or stinging cells, attached. The ascodia can be shot out of the mouth or pores in the body for protection against other anemones or predators.

Diet
Small fish, fish eggs, barnacles, crabs, mussels, chitons and sea urchins all are part of anemones' varied diet.
Enemies
The shag-rug nudibranch (p. 45), leather star (p. 76) and various fishes are known predators of sea anemones.
Reproduction
All species reproduce sexually, by releasing sperm and eggs into the ocean. The pelagic juveniles feed upon plankton until they reach a larger size. Some species also reproduce asexually, in one of two ways: longitudinal fission (the organism simply divides in two), and pedal laceration (a small portion of the pedal, or disc, is left behind when the anemone moves).
Habitat
Sites vary widely depending upon species, and include rocky and sandy shores. Both sheltered and exposed locations provide suitable habitats.

Aggregating Anemone
Anthopleura elegantissima
Key Features
Tentacles normally green with pink tips. Species often produces colonies.

Giant Green Anemone
Anthopleura xanthogrammica
Key Features
Solitary, large, green species found on exposed coasts.

Sea Anemones (Class Anthozoa)

Moonglow Anemone

Anthopleura artemisia

Key Features
Tentacles have a luminous quality, and colors vary widely from green to blue or red.

Short Plumose Anemone

Metridium senile

Key Features
White, brown or orange, with up to 100 fine tentacles.

Short plumose anemones in tidepool.

White-spotted Anemone
Urticina lofotensis
Key Features
Striking red body covered with white spots.

Stubby Rose Anemone
Urticina coriacea
Key Features
Short tentacles, banded with red and gray.

Painted Anemone
Urticina felina
Key Features
Red, green, yellow or a combination of these colors. Normally lives in sheltered locations.

Hydroids & Allies (Class Hydrozoa)

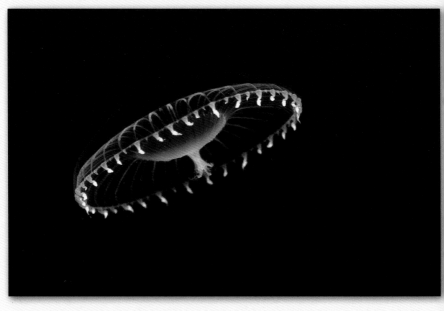

Water jelly

General Notes

Most hydrozoans live in colonies with specialized cells performing different tasks, such as the tissue required to form the nematocysts or the tissue for the branches of a hydroid. Hydroids and their allies alternate between two phases or stages in their life cycle: the polyp and the medusa. The polyp or asexual stage is the dominant form. Small jellies are among the close allies of hydroids.

Diet

This group feeds primarily on tiny planktonic animals.

Enemies

Nudibranchs are one of the main predators of hydroids. After they eat the hydroids' nematocysts, they can recycle them to help protect themselves.

Reproduction

This group reproduces both sexually, by releasing eggs and sperm into the water, and asexually, by budding from medusae.

Habitat

The sedentary members of this group require hard surfaces such as rock to attach to. Those that are not sedentary are at home in the world's oceans.

Turgid Garland Hydroid
Sertularella turgida
Key Features
Robust, yellowish, "wavy" filaments.

Wine-glass Hydroid
Obelia spp.
Key Features
Has tiny filaments shaped like wine glasses. Attaches to a wide variety of surfaces.

Ostrich-plume Hydroid
Aglaophenia spp.
Key Features
Feather-like plumes reach 6" (15 cm) tall.

**Purple
Encrusting
Hydrocoral**
Stylantheca spp.
Key Features
A purple spe-
cies that forms a
hard surface as it
encrusts rocks.

**By-the-wind
Sailor**
Velella velella
Key Features
Floating hydroid
with a distinc-
tive sail.

**Solitary
Pink-mouth
Hydroid**
*Ectopleura
marina*
Key Features
Elongated fila-
ments, distinc-
tively pink.

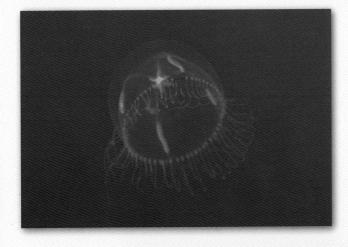

Cross Jelly
Mitrocoma cellularia
Key Features
Small jelly with a visible white cross inside.

Water Jelly
Aequorea spp.
Key Features
Small jelly with more than 100 ribs reaching 10" (25 cm) in diameter.

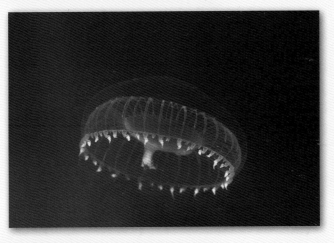

Aggregating Jelly
Eutonina indicans
Key Features
Small jelly with 4 radial canals. Grows to 1.4" (3.5 cm) in diameter.

True Jellies (Class Scyphozoa)

Lion's mane jelly

General Notes

True jellies alternate between two phases or stages: the polyp and the medusa. The medusa, or jelly-like, sexual stage is the dominant form. Individuals in this group lacks a velum (veil-like ring), which is present in members of the class Hydrozoa. The animal moves by repeatedly contracting the muscles of the bell, which pushes water out and propels the jelly forward.

Did You Know?

Some jellies are well known for being dangerous to humans. Their nematocysts contain poison that can cause a rash, an unpleasant burn or an allergic reaction if they are touched or handled. Be sure to not handle a jelly, even if it is dead and stranded on the beach.

Diet

The main diet includes zooplankton, phytoplankton, larval fish and other jellies.

Enemies

Various fishes, loggerhead turtles and various other sea creatures feed on jellies. So do humans, particularly in in Japan and China, where jellies are eaten in salads and considered a delicacy.

Reproduction

Adult jellies are either male or female. The male releases sperm from his orifice, and the sperm swim into the female's orifice to fertilize the eggs. Eventually planula (free-swimming larvae) hatch. They attach to rocks or other solid objects on the ocean floor and develop into flower-like polyps, which in turn develop into pelagic medusas.

Habitat

The medusa, the dominant form, is free-living in the world's oceans. The polyp, or sedentary form, attaches to rocks.

Lion's Mane Jelly
Cyanea capillata
Key Features
Brick red to purplish brown in color, and normally up to 20" (50 cm) in diameter.

Stranded lion's mane jelly

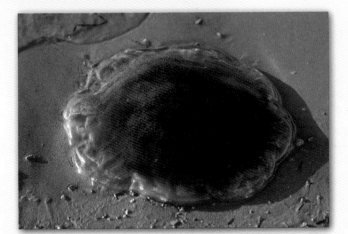

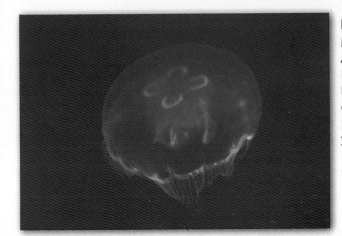

Pacific Moon Jelly
Aurelia labiata
Key Features
Normally white often with a pink, lavender or yellowish tint. Reaches 16" (40 cm) in diameter.

23

SEGMENTED WORMS

PHYLUM Annelida
The body of a segmented worm consists of many rings that are visible to the beachcomber. Inside each segment there is a repetition of organs and body parts, including the intestine and major blood vessels. Approximately 9,000 species of segmented worm have been identified worldwide. The three types or classes of these worms are Polychaeta (bristleworms), Oligochaeta (earthworms) and Hirudinea (leeches). Bristleworms, the most common group in marine environments, are discussed below.

Northern feather-duster worm colony.

Did You Know?
Segmented worms are an important food source for thousands of shorebirds on their annual migrations.

Diet
Worms' feeding styles vary widely from eating organic material that settles on a muddy substrate, to filtering plankton and detritus from the water, to preying upon a variety of small creatures.

Enemies
Many species, including birds, fishes and crabs, rely on the abundant marine worms for food.

Reproduction
In most segmented worm species the sexes are separate, but several species are hermaphrodites. Generally, both sexes release gametes into the ocean to be self-fertilized. From these eggs, microscopic larvae hatch. They feed on plankton and eventually settle onto the ocean floor, where they become juveniles. Some bristleworms can also reproduce asexually.

Habitat
Most bristleworms live in a soft medium, such as mud, but several attach to a hard surface.

Northern Feather-duster Worm
Eudistylia vancouveri
Key Features
Purple and greenish feeding tentacles. Worm is protected inside large tubes that reach 10" (25 cm) long.

Pile Worm
Nereis vexillosa
Key Features
Burrows in sand and mud. It reaches 12" (30 cm) long.

Eighteen-paired Scaleworm
Halosydna brevisetosa
Key Features
Eighteen pairs of scales cover the dorsal surface. Grows to 4.3" (11 cm) long.

MOSS ANIMALS

PHYLUM Bryozoa (or Ectoprocta)

Bryozoans produce colonies, each consisting of hundreds or thousands of individuals, called zooids. Each zooid secretes and lives inside a zooecium. These zooecia (plural) come in many different shapes and form a certain type of colony depending upon their shape. Most bryozoans are hermaphroditic—individuals have both ovaries and testes. Some species release both eggs and sperm directly into the water, where they combine, but most species brood their eggs. Bryozoans feed on fine particles present in the water. Nearly 2,000 different species are known in the world.

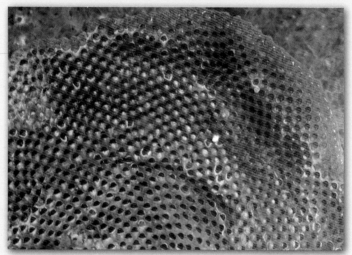

Derby hat bryozoan

Diet

This group feeds mainly on bacteria, phytoplankton and detritus, by drawing seawater through their ciliated tentacles and combing out particles of food.

Enemies

Nudibranchs (p. 42) are the main predators of bryozoans. Chitons (p. 28) and sea urchins (p. 80) are also known to feed on them.

Reproduction

Normally bryozoans are hermaphroditic, having both sexes in a colony at any one time. Colonies usually cross-fertilize with other colonies, and young are produced with a yolk-like food source. After a brief time swimming about in the plankton, individuals settle onto a surface to begin their sedentary life as a colony.

Habitat

Young bryozoans swim in the ocean for a brief period, and when they become adults, they normally attach to a hard substrate.

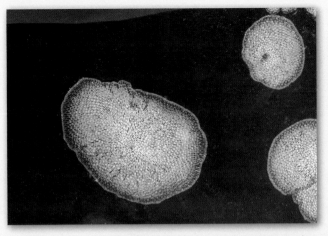

Kelp Encrusting Bryozoan
Membranipora membranacea
Key Features
A distinctive species that encrusts brown algae.

Orange Encrusting Bryozoan
Schizoporella unicornis
Key Features
Distinctive for its orange coloration.

Derby Hat Bryozoan
Eurystomella bilabiata
Key Features
Reddish in color, with derby hat-shaped apertures.

MOLLUSCS

> **PHYLUM Mollusca**
> Most molluscs (also spelled mollusks) have one or more internal or external shells, an unsegmented body, a mantle or fold in the body wall (which lines the shell or shells) and a muscular "foot." This very diverse group of creatures includes snails, nudibranchs, clams and octopuses. Scientists estimate there are as many as 130,000 species of mollusc in the world—the largest number of species in any phylum. Most of them are marine animals.

Chitons (Class Polyplacophora)

General Notes
Chitons are molluscs that are protected with eight shells, or plates, on their dorsal surface. Eyes are absent but light-sensitive organs are present on the plates. Most species shun sunlight and are nocturnal, so they are usually found in the shade or under rocks. It is estimated that a total of 600 living species of chiton occur worldwide.

Diet
Food consists of an assortment of algae and animal life, which the chiton scrapes from rocks with the radula, or rasp-like tongue.

Enemies
They are preyed upon by various fish, sea stars, ducks and river otters.

Reproduction
In most cases, male and female chitons release their gametes into the water, where fertilization occurs. A few species brood their eggs in the grooves of their foot.

Habitat
Chitons cling to rocks in the high intertidal zone and lower.

Lined Chiton
Tonicella lineata
Key Features
A colorful species whose surface is graced by zigzag lines with alternating dark and light patterns.

Mossy Chiton
Mopalia muscosa
Key Features
One of the few species frequently found in the sun. Stiff hairs grace the outer girdle.

Black Katy Chiton
Katharina tunicata
Key Features
Black, leathery outer covering with white triangle shape on each shell.

Giant Pacific Chiton
Cryptochiton stelleri
Key Features
Brick red in color, and grows to 13 inches (33 cm) in length. Plates are completely covered by the girdle.

Keyhole Limpets & Limpets (Families Fissurellidae & Acmaeidae)

Whitecap limpet

General Notes

True limpets have a single cone-shaped shell with no perforations. Keyhole limpets are similar in shape with a perforation at the apex, or tip, of the shell. In both groups the shell protects the body with a large muscular foot on which they move about. Some species have a "home scar"—a depression in the rock that they always return to at low tide.

Diet

Most keyhole limpets and limpets feed on algae, mainly microscopic algae. The animals scrape food from rock surfaces with the radula, or rasp-like tongue.

Enemies

A range of predators, including fish, crabs and a variety of birds, feed on these creatures by breaking their shells.

Reproduction

Limpets shed their gametes into the sea for fertilization. The fertilized eggs develop into pelagic, or free-swimming, larvae.

Habitat

Most keyhole limpets and limpets live on hard rock surfaces between the high and low intertidal zones.

Rough Keyhole Limpet
Diodora aspera
Key Features
Large shell with small circular opening at the apex.

Two-spot Keyhole Limpet
Fissurellidea bimaculata
Key Features
Small shell with a large, elongated opening at the apex.

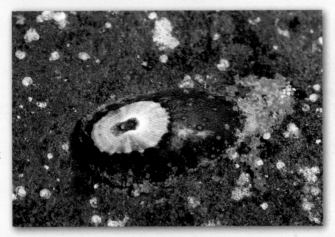

Whitecap Limpet
Acmaea mitra
Key Features
White or pink, with a very high cone-shaped shell.

Ribbed Limpet
Lottia digitalis
Key Features
Elliptical shell with several rather prominent ribs that radiate from the apex.

Pacific Plate Limpet
Lottia scutum
Key Features
Very flat shell, rather thin in young individuals.

Mask Limpet
Lottia persona
Key Features
Stout, somewhat high shell with a noticeable hook near the apex.

Shield Limpet
Lottia pelta
Key Features
Somewhat high shell, often with a wavy edge.

Shell interior of shield limpet.

Shell interior of fenestrate limpet.

Fenestrate Limpet
Lottia fenestrata
Key Features
Apex often eroded to brown. A dark interior is often present.

Snails

There are several types of snails present in the Pacific Northwest, most of which have coiled shells. Each group is discussed separately.

Periwinkles (Family Littorinidae)

Sitka periwinkle

General Notes

Periwinkles are small snails, some of which spend most of their time out of water. Two species are commonly encountered in the Pacific Northwest, and they are often found together on beaches. Larger individuals frequent higher intertidal levels, likely because they are less susceptible to desiccation.

Did you know?

In Europe, a large species of periwinkle is eaten by humans. The common periwinkle *Littorina littorea*, also known as escargot, is not as popular as it once was.

Diet

Principal sources of food include diatoms and certain algae such as sea lettuce and black seaside lichen.

Enemies

The northern striped dogwinkle (p. 39), mottled star (p. 75), six-rayed star (p. 76), northern clingfish (p. 89), glaucous-winged gull and surf scoter are known predators of periwinkles.

Reproduction

Females deposit eggs, which, depending on the species, hatch into either planktonic veligers (larvae) or miniature versions of the adult.

Habitat

Periwinkles are found on rock surfaces, algae and similar areas in the splash zone to mid-intertidal zone.

Sitka Periwinkle
Littorina sitkana
Key Features
Round shell, black or very dark purple in color, is adorned with spiral ridges and grooves. May have bands of white, yellow or orange.

Checkered Periwinkle
Littorina scutulata
Key Features
Smooth, elongated shell, black or very dark purple with light spots in a checkerboard pattern.

This checkered periwinkle is opening its operculum (trapdoor).

Top Snails & Turbans (Families Trochidae & Turbinidae)

General Notes
The snails in these families have a top-shaped shell. The whorls may be flattened or rounded, depending upon the species.

Diet
Most members of this clan are herbivorous—feeding on algae and detritus. They may also take a few very small organisms with the algae they scrape from rock. The shell of many species has a beautiful mother-of-pearl finish on the inside.

Enemies
Sea stars (p. 74), some species of fish and sea ducks are known to feed on top snails and turbans.

Reproduction
The sexes are separate, and fertilization takes place internally. Females produce eggs, which are shed into the water and eventually develop into juvenile snails.

Habitat
The habitat varies quite a lot from species to species in this group. Some prefer exposed rocky shorelines, while others inhabit kelp forests.

Dusky turban in tidepool.

Blue Topsnail
Calliostoma ligatum
Key Features
Small blue snail with many brown spiral ridges circling the shell.

Black Turban
Chlorostoma funebralis
Key Features
A large species, black overall, often with a "bald" spot on the top.

Dusky Turban
Promartynia pulligo
Key Features
A large species, brown overall, with an open umbilicus ("navel").

Dogwinkles (Family Nucellidae)

This frilled dogwinkle has a smooth shell.

General Notes

Dogwinkles are common predators that occupy the intertidal zone. They are very abundant in some places.

Diet

The diet of dogwinkles includes barnacles, limpets, mussels and other snails.

Enemies

Dogwinkles are considered the main course for various sea stars, especially the purple star (p. 75) and the red rock crab (p. 70).

Reproduction

Male and female dogwinkles reproduce by internal fertilization. The female deposits eggs, which develop directly into miniature adults. Some species produce nurse eggs—eggs that contain no fertilized embryo and are used to feed the young that hatch. The female frilled dogwinkle is noteworthy for her penis, which is half the size of the male's.

Habitat

Dogwinkles live in rocky intertidal habitats.

Frilled Dogwinkle

Nucella lamellosa

Key Features
Elongated shell varies greatly —smooth in exposed areas but frilled in quiet, sheltered locations.

Northern Striped Dogwinkle

Nucella ostrina

Key Features
Smooth, rounded shell that varies greatly in color and often has stripes.

Channelled Dogwinkle

Nucella canaliculata

Key Features
Rounded shell, covered with grooved channels.

Additional Snails

Leafy Hornmouth
Ceratostoma foliatum
Key Features
Ornate shell, adorned with three leaf-like frills.

Dire Whelk
Lirabuccinum dirum
Key Features
Bluish-gray shell, covered with numerous spiral threads. Aperture extends over more than half the shell.

Purple Olive
Olivella biplicata
Key Features
Striking white to dark purple shell. Burrows near the surface on sandy beaches.

Lewis's Moonsnail
Euspira lewisii
Key Features
Large, rounded shell reaching 5.5" (14 cm) in height. Encloses a massive foot.

Wrinkled Amphissa
Amphissa columbiana
Key Features
Yellow to pink shell with several longitudinal whorls.

Mudflat Snail
Batillaria attramentaria
Key Features
Small, elongated shell. Found in mudflats.

Nudibranchs (Order Nudibranchia)

Red nudibranch

General Notes

Nudibranchs are soft-bodied marine slugs that have no shell when they are adults. Many are very distinctive creatures decorated with all colors of the rainbow. Several types of nudibranchs inhabit Pacific Northwest waters. Dorid nudibranchs have plumes that form a cluster near the rear. Other nudibranchs produce finger-like extensions on the dorsal surface, with which the animal breathes and digests food. In other species these functions are performed within the body. More than 3,000 nudibranch species have been described around the world. They range in size from microscopic to 16" (40 cm) long, but most reach about 4" (10 cm) long.

Diet

Collectively, nudibranchs consume an amazing array of life forms, but most of them feed on a single type of marine plant or animal per species. The red nudibranch, for example, only eats encrusting sponges, while an adult barnacle-eating dorid only feeds on barnacles.

Enemies

Nudibranchs have few known enemies. They taste bad, which protects them very well, and some possess nematocysts (stinging cells). They also have short lives—most individuals live less than one year.

Reproduction

Nudibranchs are hermaphrodites, having both male and female reproductive organs. Each individual produces both sperm and eggs simultaneously, and when they mate, they fertilize each other, one taking on the male role and the other a female role. Egg masses are deposited and either miniature adults or planktonic veligers (free-swimming larvae) emerge.

Habitat

Nudibranchs live on a wide variety of surfaces in the intertidal zone and lower.

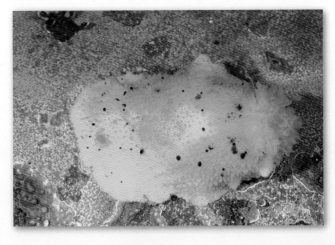

Monterey Dorid
Doris montereyensis
Key Features
Yellow with dark projections on the body and yellowish gills near the rear.

Sea Lemon
Peltodoris nobilis
Key Features
Yellow with dark markings between projections on the body and white gills near the rear.

Red Nudibranch
Rostanga pulchra
Key Features
A unique intertidal dorid, red to tan overall.

Additional Nudibranchs

Barnacle-eating Dorid
Onchidoris bilamellata
Key Features
Mottled brown body. Found in the mid-intertidal zone with barnacles.

Rufus Tipped Nudibranch
Acanthodoris nanaimoensis
Key Features
Yellow-tipped projections covering the body, but rufus present on tips of the gills and rhinophores (organs of smell).

Opalescent Nudibranch
Hermissenda crassicornis
Key Features
Gray body with numerous projections, orange line down the center and blue lines to the left and right.

Ringed Nudibranch
Diaulula sandiegensis
Key Features
Light brown in color with dark brown rings or spots.

Frosted Nudibranch
Dirona albolineata
Key Features
Numerous gray, purplish or salmon-colored projections covering the body, each highlighted with a white line.

Shag-rug Nudibranch
Aeolidia papillosa
Key Features
Many brownish cerata (projections) covering the body, with a "bald" spot at the center.

Clams and Allies (Class Bivalvia)

Clams and their allies have 2 valves or shells as well as being bilaterally symmetrical. The valves protect the body of the animal but allow the siphons and foot to protrude if both are present. Depending on the species, the siphons may barely protrude, or may extend a considerable distance to reach the surface of the substrate. It is estimated that there are about 10,000 species of bivalves living in the world.

Mussels (Family Mytilidae)

General Notes
Mussels are elongated bivalves that produce a byssus, or byssal threads—thin yet strong threads, produced by a gland located in the foot, that anchor the animal to a rock surface. Mussels have no hinge teeth. One species, the California mussel, can produce pearls, but they have no commercial value.

Mussel beds where harvesting takes place are monitored for pollution over a wide area to detect the presence of toxic algae blooms, which can be harmful to people. Red tide is the most common of these toxins. Monitoring information is relevant to the harvest of all species of bivalves in the area.

Did You Know?
The Pacific blue mussel can sometimes protect itself from attacking predatory snails in a very interesting way. When a dogwinkle or other attacking snail gets too close, the mussel can stick byssal threads to the snail's shell and quickly attach these threads to a rock or other solid object, thereby restraining the snail. The predator becomes anchored down and usually dies.

Diet
Mussels draw in seawater and filter out phytoplankton, detritus and other food.

Enemies
Predators of mussels include large anemones, various sea stars, carnivorous snails, fish and a variety of birds. Indeed, this species is an important food for a wide range of organisms—including human beings.

Reproduction
In the Pacific Northwest, spawning occurs during summer and fall. Eggs are spawned and fertilized, then quickly develop into pelagic veligers (larvae). Eventually the young mussels settle on solid objects to begin the sedentary stage of their life.

Habitat
Rocks, wharves and similar surfaces provide excellent sites for mussels to attach.

Pacific blue mussels

California Mussel
Mytilus californianus
Key Features
A large species reaching 10″ (25 cm) long. Common on surf-exposed shores.

Pacific Blue Mussel
Mytilus trossulus
Key Features
Reaches 4.5″ (11 cm). Common at sheltered locations.

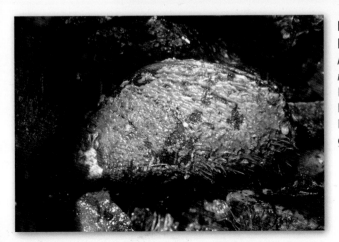

Northern Horsemussel
Modiolus modiolus
Key Features
Brownish shell. Burrows in gravel.

Oysters (Family Ostreidae)

Pacific oysters

General Notes

Oysters have two unequal shells, one of which is normally attached to a rock or other hard surface. Oysters do not produce byssal threads, and no foot is present.

Did You Know?

Oysters have been considered a delicacy for countless years. The oyster is also consumed as an aphrodisiac, and researchers have recently found that this may be true—oysters are rich in rare amino acids that do trigger the release of sex hormones. To be effective, though, they must be eaten raw!

Diet

Oysters are filter feeders that draw plankton (microscopic food) from the water.

Enemies

Humans, various sea stars, carnivorous snails and crabs are the primary predators of oysters.

Reproduction

Oysters are hermaphroditic. All individuals begin as males, and they later transform into females. A large female oyster may release more than 100 million eggs in one season, but only about 1 percent of these mature to the next stage. The larvae go through several stages before they settle into the sedentary stage.

Habitat

Sheltered rocky shores are the preferred habitat for most oysters. They also settle on boats and other oysters. When they settle on other oysters, they are collectively called an "oyster reef."

Pacific Oyster
Crassostrea gigas
Key Features
Large species with a fluted exterior edge. Reaches 12" (30 cm) in length.

Olympia Oyster
Ostrea conchaphila
Key Features
Small and round, or elongated. Reaches 3.5" (8.8 cm) in length.

Scallops (Family Pectinidae)

Giant rock scallop

General Notes
Most scallops lie on the ocean bottom with the right valve (shell) down. That lower valve is normally lighter in color than the other. Some adult scallops are free swimming, moving through the water by performing a repeated "clapping" movement with their valves. The giant rock scallop is free swimming early in its life but later cements one valve to a hard surface. A small scallop fishery takes place on the Pacific coast.

Did You Know?
A scallop has several eyes on its mantle. These are not used to see images but rather to detect shadows—perhaps predators.

Diet
Like all bivalves, scallops filter their food from the water. Their diet consists of phytoplankton.

Enemies
Various sea stars and birds such as the white-winged scoter are known predators in the Pacific Northwest.

Reproduction
Normally the sexes are separate, and ocean-going veligers (larvae) develop from the eggs.

Habitat
Many scallops live on rocky bottoms, but some, such as the smooth pink scallop, prefer soft bottoms.

**Smooth
Pink Scallop**
Chlamys rubida
Key Features
Outer surface of
shell is smooth.

**Spiny
Pink Scallop**
Chlamys hastata
Key Features
Outer surface of
shell is spiny.

**Giant
Rock Scallop**
*Crassadoma
gigantea*
Key Features
Shell is often
distorted. In ma-
ture individuals,
shell is also very
thick and heavy.

Clams

Shells of the bent-nose macoma.

General Notes
Clams comprise several families of bivalves that possess a foot and a pair of siphons. The incurrent siphon brings water and food into the mantle, and the excurrent siphon expels waste and filtered water. These siphons may be fused together or separate, depending upon the species. The foot anchors the animal in the sand or mud.

Diet
Bivalves filter seawater, combing out detritus, diatoms and other minute food particles suspended in the water.

Enemies
The Lewis's moonsnail (see p. 41) preys on these species. Small clams may become dinner for birds, including the American wigeon or semipalmated sandpiper, and the siphons may be nipped off by various fish, crabs and shrimp.

Reproduction
Mature individuals swim freely in spring and summer to spawn. They produce fertilized eggs that develop into pelagic veligers (larvae). The young eventually settle onto soft bottoms to begin their more sedentary life beneath the surface of the sand or mud.

Habitat
Most clams prefer sand, mud or a mixture of both. Some species live in gravel beds.

Bent-nose Macoma
Macoma nasuta
Key Features
Shells are bent to the right.

White-sand Macoma
Macoma secta
Key Features
Elongated shells, white on exterior with fine concentric lines.

Baltic Macoma
Macoma balthica
Key Features
Small shells, often pinkish in color.

Additional Clams

Fat Gaper
Tresus capax
Key Features
Large, heavy,
oval shells with a
gape.

Pacific Gaper
Tresus nuttallii
Key Features
Large, heavy,
elongated shells
with a gape.

*Siphons of the
Pacific gaper.*

Nuttall's Cockle
Clinocardium nuttallii
Key Features
Thick shells with strong ribs and a heart-shaped cross-section.

Purple Mahogany-clam
Nuttallia obscurata
Key Features
Rich mahogany brown shells with deep purple interior.

California Sunset Clam
Gari californica
Key Features
White shells, often with pink rays, covered with a thin periostracum (skin-like coating).

Favorite Eating Clams

Did You Know?
If you harvest clams, be sure to check with local officials to ensure that the area is free from paralytic shellfish poisoning, or PSP—also known as red tide. This and other poisons are monitored throughout the Pacific Northwest to make sure shellfish are safe to eat. See page 8 for hotlines from Alaska to California.

Softshell-clam
Mya arenaria
Key Features
Thin shells. Spoon-shaped chondrophore (projection) on inside of left shell.

Pacific Razor-clam
Siliqua patula
Key Features
Thin rectangular shells with varnish-like finish.

To capture the Pacific razor-clam, look for a dimple in the sand.

Pacific Littleneck
Protothaca staminea
Key Features
Round shells with rough inside margin.

Japanese Littleneck
Venerupis philippinarum
Key Features
Elongated shells with smooth inside margin.

Butter Clam
Saxidomus gigantea
Key Features
Large, heavy shells with several concentric lines.

57

Rock Borers (Family Pholadidae)

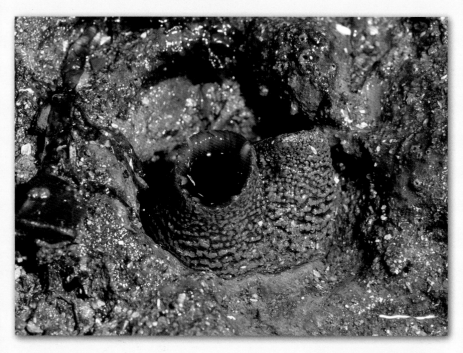

Siphons of rough piddock.

General Notes

Piddocks are bivalves that often make their homes inside rock. These amazing creatures can actually drill into soft rock, concrete or clay to make a cavity large enough to live in. The process is a life-long activity of enlarging the burrow as the animal grows. Some species, such as the rough piddock, dig by rotating their shells, and others use a rocking motion.

Diet

Piddocks obtain their food by drawing in water through the inhalant siphon and filtering out minute particles and plankton.

Enemies

Flatworms enter the shells, eat the flesh and lay their eggs inside. Various sea stars are also likely enemies of piddocks.

Reproduction

The flat-tip piddock produces planktonic larvae, which later settle on the bottom and begin their "boring" life.

Habitat

Hard clay, shale, sandstone, concrete are all substrates for these bivalves to carve out their dwellings.

Boring Softshell-clam
Platyodon cancellatus
Key Features
Rectangular shells. Exterior has one section.

Flat-tip Piddock
Penitella penita
Key Features
Elongated wedge-shaped shells. Exterior has 3 separate sections.

Rough Piddock
Zirfaea pilsbryi
Key Features
Short, oval shells. Exterior has 2 separate sections.

59

ARTHROPODS

> **PHYLUM Arthropoda**
>
> Arthropods are a large group of diverse creatures with "jointed feet" as well as an exoskeleton (a skeleton that covers the body) that is made of chitin. Some arthropods, such as spiders, do not live in a marine environment. Those species that are marine include barnacles, isopods, amphipods, shrimps and crabs. It has been estimated that more than 900,000 living species of arthropods are present in the world, and many fossil species as well.

Barnacles (Class Cirripedia)

General Notes

Barnacles can be separated into two groups: barnacles and goose barnacles. The goose barnacle has a flexible stalk to support the rest of the body. Barnacles are protected by calcareous shells that are attached to a hard object such as a rock. Some barnacles are parasitic on whales, crabs or sea stars.

Did You Know?

Barnacles use their legs to gather their food! The feather-like legs, called cirri, have been modified for food gathering.

Diet

Barnacles feed upon small plants, animals and organic matter that are present in the water column. They collect this food by sweeping their feathery cirri through the water.

Enemies

Whelks (predatory snails), sea stars (p. 74), fish and shorebirds feed on barnacles.

Reproduction

All barnacles are hermaphroditic (both male and female). They transfer the sperm from one individual to another through a very long penis. The eggs are brooded, then released into the water. There they pass through two stages in their metamorphosis before attaching to a solid object for the rest of their lives.

Habitat

During the sedentary part of its life, the barnacle attaches itself to a float, rock, shell or similar object, depending upon the species.

Acorn barnacle feeding underwater.

Thatched Barnacle
Semibalanus cariosus
Key Features
Grayish, volcano-shaped shells covered with several downward-pointing spines.

Acorn Barnacle
Balanus glandula
Key Features
Small, smooth gray or white shells.

Goose Barnacle
Pollicipes polymerus
Key Features
Long, flexible stalk holds the gray or bluish plates.

Isopods (Order Isopoda)

General Notes
Isopod simply means "equal foot," referring to its legs, which are approximately equal in size. An individual in this group normally has 7 pairs of legs and a body that is flattened dorsoventrally (from top to bottom). Approximately 4,500 marine species are known to inhabit the world's oceans.

Vosnesensky's isopod

Diet
The diet of isopods varies greatly depending on the species. Some are carnivores, others feed on vegetation, detritus or wood, and still others are parasitic.

Enemies
Various fishes are known to be major predators of isopods.

Reproduction
The sexes are separate in the isopods, and they do not undergo a planktonic stage. Instead, young are brooded in a brood pouch, from which miniature versions of the adults then emerge.

Habitat
Members of this group often live among algae or under rocks.

Scavenging Isopod

Cirolana harfordi

Key Features
Gray to brown or black body, graced with 2 flattened appendages on the abdomen.

Monterey Isopod
Idotea montereyensis
Key Features
A narrow body graced with a small projection on a rounded abdomen.

Vosnesensky's Isopod
Idotea wosnesenskii
Key Features
A large species, growing to 1.4" (3.6 cm). Cryptically colored with green or brown. Tip of abdomen is rounded with a small projection.

Sea Slater
Ligia pallasii
Key Features
A cockroach-like isopod that lives in the spray zone.

Amphipods (Order Amphipoda)

General Notes

Amphipods come in a wide variety of shapes and sizes, but most are elongated with C-shaped bodies that are flattened laterally (from side to side). Their bodies have 3 regions: head, thorax and abdomen. Two pairs of antennae are present, both well developed and unbranched. The thorax has 8 pairs of appendages, and the abdomen has 6 pairs of appendages.

Diet

Amphipods feed on plants and small animals, or they scavenge dead bodies. One group lives on the exterior of marine mammals and feeds on their skin. Other groups of amphipods have even more specialized diets.

Enemies

Fishes are the primary predators of many amphipods. In fact, amphipods are the main item in many fishes' diets.

Reproduction

The sexes are separate. The male transfers sperm directly to the female, which brood the eggs in a pouch under the thorax. Since the young are not pelagic, newly hatched amphipods look very similar to the adults.

Habitat

Most amphipods live in among detritus, or in burrows of mud. Some live on the beach among sand grains, and others live associated with jellies or tunicates.

Pink Beach Hopper
Maera danae
Key Features
The body is pink. Common in tidepools.

California Beach Hopper
Megalorchestia californiana
Key Features
Large antennae, bright orange or red.

Blue Beach Hopper
Megalorchestia Columbiana
Key Features
Bluish overall with "butterfly" markings on the dorsal surface.

Skeleton Shrimp
Caprella spp.
Key Features
Resembles a miniature shrimp.

Shrimps (Order Decapoda)

General Notes
Shrimps and crabs belong to the Order Decapoda and are closely related to each other. Shrimps have laterally compressed bodies and very slender walking legs. Approximately 1,700 living species of shrimp have been identified around the world.

Did You Know?
Shrimps have enormous abdominal muscles that they use to escape from predators, by jerking the tail fan beneath the body. These muscles are the bulk of the shrimp that we enjoy eating.

Diet
The menu of the shrimp clan includes amphipods (see p. 64), other shrimp and bristleworms (p. 24). Shrimps are also scavengers of carcasses.

Enemies
Cormorants, various fishes and the giant octopus are known to feed on shrimps. Humans are also a main predator.

Reproduction
Most shrimp are protandric hermaphrodites: males that later change into females. As well, most species' life cycle includes a stage of pelagic young. A few, however, brood their eggs, which develop directly into miniature adults.

Habitat
Most shrimps inhabit rocky shorelines, but several species are at home on sandy beaches.

Stout Shrimp
Heptacarpus brevirostris
Key Features
Large and stout, with 5 or 6 dorsal spines on the carapace and a flattened nose-like rostrum.

Smooth Bay Shrimp
Lissocrangon stylirostris
Key Features
Slender body. Settles just under the surface of the sand.

Bay Ghost Shrimp
Neotrypaea californiensis
Key Features
Pink or yellowish, with one large claw. Builds a burrow in the sand.

Blue Mud Shrimp
Upogebia pugettensis
Key Features
Bluish gray body with 2 equal claws. Builds a burrow in the sand and mud.

Crabs

General Notes

The several groups of crabs include true crabs, hermit crabs and many other families—in fact, there are more than 50 families of crabs. Each family has particular distinguishing characteristics. True crabs, for instance, have 5 pairs of walking legs, all about the same size, and a hard abdomen.

Diet

Crabs feed on a wide variety of organisms, including various algae and animal matter.

Enemies

Fishes prey on many species of crabs, and octopus, ribbon worms and amphipods (p. 64) feed on the eggs of some species.

Reproduction

As in all crustaceans, the sexes are separate in crabs. The female normally lays her eggs shortly after mating, and the eggs are brooded while they are attached to the female's abdomen. Tiny larvae then hatch. They swim in the plankton and moult several times until reaching a stage where they settle on the sea floor.

Habitat

Crabs inhabit a wide variety of environments, most often rocky or sandy shores.

Hermit Crabs

Grainyhand Hermit
Pagurus granosimanus
Key Features
Solid orange antennae. Body covered with white or blue spots.

Hairy Hermit
Pagurus hirsutiusculus
Key Features
Brown antennae with bands. Single white band on each leg.

Greenmark Hermit
Pagurus caurinus
Key Features
Solid red antennae, and white bands on the legs.

Blueband Hermit
Pagurus samuelis
Key Features
Blue bands circle on each leg.

69

Edible Crabs

Did You Know?
The male Dungeness crab uses pheromones (chemical scents) to find a female. Once he finds one, he mates and remains with her for up to 2 days.

Harvesting Crabs
If you plan to harvest crabs, be sure to check the limits for each species. Harvest only males so females are left for breeding.

Red Rock Crab
Cancer productus
Key Features
Black tips normally on claws. D-shaped carapace to 7" (18 cm) wide. Prefers rocky areas.

This red rock crab lacks black tips on its claws.

Dungeness Crab
Cancer magister
Key Features
White tips on claws, carapace to 9" (22.5 cm) wide. Prefers sandy areas.

Male dungeness crab.

Female dungeness crab.

71

Additional Crabs

Flattop Crab
*Petrolisthes
eriomerus*
Key Features
A porcelain crab
with blue mouth-
parts and a blue
spot at the base
of the movable
portion of each
claw.

Flat
Porcelain Crab
*Petrolisthes
cinctipes*
Key Features
Red mouthparts
and a red spot at
the base of the
movable portion
of each claw.

Shield-backed
Kelp Crab
*Pugettia
producta*
Key Features
Distinctive
shield-shaped
shell. Often
found on or near
kelp.

European Green Crab
Carcinus maenas
Key Features
An introduced species, usually green overall, with 5 large teeth on each side of its carapace.

Green Shore Crab
Hemigrapsus oregonensis
Key Features
A small crab, usually green or yellow, with fine hairs on its legs.

Purple Shore Crab
Hemigrapsus nudus
Key Features
A small crab with no hairs on its legs. Often has purple spots on its claws.

SPINY-SKINNED ANIMALS

Sea Stars (Class Asteroidea)

PHYLUM Echinodermata

Spiny-skinned animals, or echinoderms, have a soft layer of skin that covers an internal skeleton made of calcareous plates. Tentacle-like structures called tube feet are also present on all species in this phylum, and adults exhibit radial symmetry. The animals in this large group have amazing powers of regeneration.

General Notes

Sea stars have five or more distinct arms, or rays, with pedicellariae (small pinching structures) and tube feet present on the underside of each arm. Sea stars move by using their tube feet. The common term starfish is not generally accepted, since members of this group are not related to fish. It has been estimated that approximately 1,500 living species of sea stars inhabit the world.

Diet

Many sea stars are carnivorous predators of mussels, clams, limpets, chitons and other molluscs. Some species consume sponges and other sea stars.

Enemies

Gulls are the main predator of small sea stars. Some species prey on other sea stars.

Reproduction

The sexes are separate, with gonads present on each arm of a sea star. Gametes are released into the ocean, where they are fertilized. Larvae then hatch, and they feed on plankton. A few species release large, yolk-filled eggs, which are brooded by the female.

Habitat

Rocky shores are the most common environment of sea stars.

This Pacific blood star will regenerate its missing arm.

Purple Star
Pisaster ochraceus
Key Features
A very common species, normally purple or orange, with a patterned surface.

Mottled Star
Evasterias troschelii
Key Features
Brown to orange, often mottled with slender arms.

Pacific Blood Star
Henricia leviuscula
Key Features
Red to orange body with very slender arms.

Additional Sea Stars

Did You Know?
The sunflower star is the fastest sea star in the Pacific Northwest, and possibly the entire world!

Leather Star
Dermasterias imbricata
Key Features
Reddish brown to orange-brown body with a slippery surface.

Bat Star
Asterina miniata
Key Features
Comes in a wide variety of colors, with short, broad webbed arms.

Delicate Six-rayed Star
Leptasterias aequalis
(species complex)
Key Features
Brightly colored with 6 arms. Includes several species.

Morning Sun Star
Solaster dawsoni
Key Features
Uniformly yellow, gray, brown or red body, with 8 to 15 arms.

Striped Sun Star
Solaster stimpsoni
Key Features
A total of 9 or 10 arms, each with a purple or blue stripe.

Sunflower Star
Pycnopodia helianthoides
Key Features
Covered with a soft skin. Normally 24 arms.

SPINY-SKINNED ANIMALS

Brittle Stars (Class Ophiuroidea)

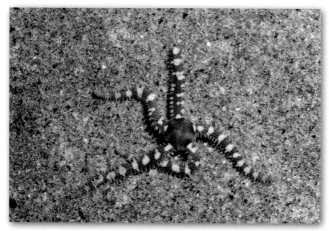

Daisy brittle star

General Notes
Brittle stars are distinctive for their very long, slender arms being separate from their central disc.

Diet
Most brittle stars feed on detritus or scavenge on dead animals. Some species actively feed on small animals and diatoms.

Enemies
Brittle stars are prey to various fish, crabs and sea stars—their close relatives.

Reproduction
In most species the sexes are separate. Some species produce large numbers of eggs, which are released into the ocean and become ocean-going larvae. Other species produce many fewer but larger eggs, which are brooded by the mother. Young stars that are brooded do not go through a pelagic stage.

Habitat
Since brittle stars avoid sunlight, most species are normally found under rocks or other such objects. A few species burrow into sand.

Dwarf Brittle Star
Amphipholis squamata
Key Features
A tiny species with a round central disc without bulges.

Daisy Brittle Star
Ophiopholis aculeate
Key Features
A common species with a central disc and bulges between the arms.

Long-armed Brittle Star
Amphiodia occidentalis
Key Features
Very long arms. Often burrows in sand and mud.

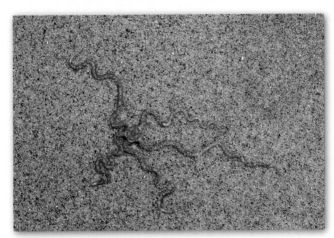

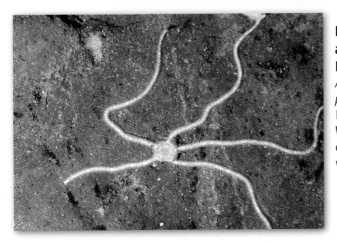

Black and White Brittle Star
Amphipholis pugetana
Key Features
White to gray, or banded with white to grey.

Sea Urchins & Sand Dollars (Class Echinoidea)

General Notes

Sea urchins and sand dollars have disc-like bodies that may be globular or flattened. They do not have arms (rays). Pincers on stalks cover much of the body. Approximately 800 species are known to live in the world.

Did You Know?

Purple sea urchins often use their sharp spines to erode shallow burrows in soft rock. Large areas of rock can be affected by this activity.

Diet

Sea urchins feed on various seaweeds as well as animal matter. Sand dollars feed on seaweeds.

Enemies

The many enemies of sea urchins include sea stars, various fish, crabs, sea otters and humans. Sea urchins are harvested in several commercial fisheries along the Pacific coast. The primary predators of sand dollars are fishes and sea stars.

Reproduction

The sexes are typically separate. Gametes are broadcast into the water, where they are fertilized. The eggs develop into pelagic larvae, which feed on plankton and eventually metamorphose and settle to the bottom to begin life as juvenile urchins. Female sand dollars can produce up to 379,000 eggs per year.

Habitat

Rocky shores are the ideal sites for most sea urchins. Sand dollars require sandy shores as habitat.

Test

**Eccentric
Sand Dollar**
Dendraster excentricus
Key Features
Flat and coin-shaped.
Lives on sandy shores.

Green Sea Urchin

Strongylocentrotus droebachiensis

Key Features
Green, relatively short spines.

Purple Sea Urchin

Strongylocentrotus purpuratus

Key Features
Short purple spines, reaching 1" (2.5 cm) in length.

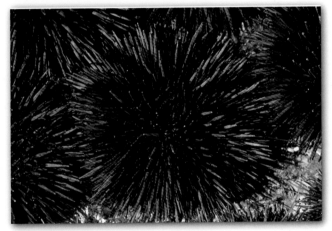

Red Sea Urchin

Strongylocentrotus franciscanus

Key Features
Red or purple spines, always long, reaching 2.75" (7 cm) in length.

Sea Cucumbers (Class Holothuroidea)

Feeding tentacles of California sea cucumber.

General Notes

Sea cucumbers are soft-bodied echinoderms. The body has a mouth opening at one end and an anus at the other. Tube feet around the mouth region are modified for feeding, and tube feet on the outer body are used for locomotion.

Diet

Sea cucumbers are filter-feeders, gathering detritus and small organisms that are suspended in seawater.

Enemies

Various sea stars (p. 74) and humans are predators of sea cucumbers.

Reproduction

Normally the sexes are separate, and each sex releases gametes into the seawater for fertilization and the early stages of growth. Some sea cucumbers brood their eggs.

Habitat

Most members of this group live under rocks or burrow into mud or other soft mediums.

California Sea Cucumber
Parastichopus californicus
Key Features
A large, reddish brown species, to 20" (50 cm) long.

Orange Sea Cucumber
Cucumaria miniata
Key Features
Elongated orange body with 10 feeding tentacles at the feeding end.

Stiff-footed Sea Cucumber
Eupentacta quinquesemita
Key Features
White body with stiff tube feet.

TUNICATES

PHYLUM Chordata

Chordates comprise two large groups: non-vertebrate chordates and vertebrate chordates. Tunicates, or sea squirts, are non-vertebrate chordates that were formerly included in the Phylum Urochordata, which is now classified as a subphylum. Vertebrate chordates include fishes, mammals, birds and others that have vertebrae.

Tunicates (Class Ascidiacea)

General Notes

Tunicates, also called sea squirts or ascidians, are chordates—animals that have a notochord. Larval tunicates have a notochord in the tail area, while adults do not. Tunicates have an incurrent siphon for respiration and for drawing in water for food, and an excurrent siphon to expel water, waste and non-food particles. Tunicates may be solitary or colonial. Solitary species are often large and separate from other individuals. Colonial species are much smaller and live in groups, sometimes with many individuals. Colonial tunicates may be social (joined by a common connection at the base) or compound (fused, sharing both a tunic and an excurrent siphon).

Did You Know?

Some tunicates can draw vanadium, a metal element, from seawater and concentrate it in their bodies. The purpose or advantage of this is unknown.

Diet

Tunicates consume small particles in the water, including bacteria, diatoms, detritus and the larvae of various invertebrates.

Enemies

Predatory snails, crabs, sea stars, worms and othe creatures are known to feed on species in this group.

Reproduction

Most species are hermaphroditic (male and female simultaneously), but they rarely self-fertilize.

Habitat

Sea squirts live on hard surfaces such as rock, boat hulls and floating docks.

Solitary Sea Squirts

Spiny-headed Sea Squirt
Boltenia villosa
Key Features
Red, tan or orange body covered with spines.

Stalked Sea Squirt
Styela montereyensis
Key Features
Elongated, corrugated body on a short stalk.

Shiny Red Sea Squirt
Cnemidocarpa finmarkiensis
Key Features
Smooth, red surface. Body deflates when out of water.

Social (Colonial) Tunicates

Taylor's Social Tunicate
Metandrocarpa taylori
Key Features
Orange, red or yellow individual tunics, .25" (6 mm) in diameter.

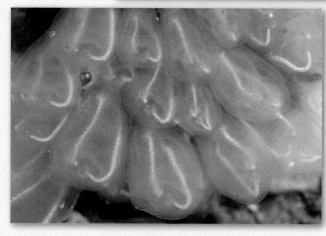

Lightbulb Tunicate
Clavelina huntsmani
Key Features
Distinctive species forming light bulb shapes.

Compound (Colonial) Tunicates

Red Sea Pork
Aplidium solidum
Key Features
Thick reddish slab that encrusts rocks.

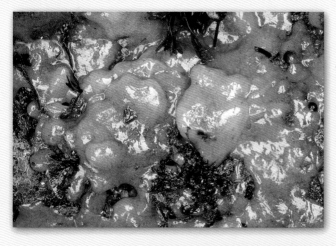

California Sea Pork
Aplidium californicum
Key Features
Yellowish to orange encrusting slabs.

Mushroom Tunicate
Distaplia occidentalis
Key Features
White to pink or purple. Several individuals combine in larger units.

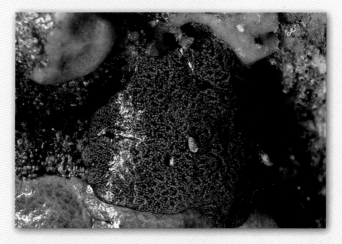

Harbour Star Ascidian
Botryllus schlosseri
Key Features
Distinctive species forming flower-shaped clusters.

FISHES

PHYLUM Chordata
Fishes are vertebrate chordates. All species have an internal skeleton and most are covered in scales. Approximately 21,000 species are present in the world.

Bony Fishes (Class Osteichthyes)

Did you know?
Fishes are the most diverse and successful vertebrate group, comprising more than half of all vertebrates living today.

Diet
The diet of fishes varies considerably with species. There are herbivores (plant eaters), carnivores (meat eaters), omnivores (plant and meat eaters) and detritivores (eaters of decomposing plants and animals). Fishes feed on annelid worms, marine snails, mussels, clams, squids, crustaceans, insects, birds, amphibians, small mammals and other fishes.

Enemies
The main enemy of fishes is larger fishes.

Reproduction
In most species of bony fishes, the sperm and eggs develop in separate male and female individuals. The adults release unfertilized eggs and sperm, and the young develop from eggs that are fertilized in water.

Habitat
Most intertidal fishes live among algae, under rocks or in similar situations.

Tidepool Sculpin
Oligocottus maculosus
Key Features
Greenish to brownish in color. Commonly found in tide-pools.

Crescent Gunnel
Pholis laeta
Key Features
The long body is slender. Crescent shape present through the eye.

Northern Clingfish
Gobiesox maeandricus
Key Features
Large adhesive disk on the belly. Commonly found under rocks.

Plainfin Midshipman
Porichthys notatus
Key Features
Large species with tiny dorsal fin and no spotting on the fins.

Glossary

Acontia: Thin threads that contain nematocysts. They are emitted defensively by many anemones.

Aeolid: A type of nudibranch that has cerata rather than a plume-like gill on its back.

Antenna (plural Antennae): A slender sensory appendage that projects from the head area.

Aperture: The opening into which the entire body of a snail can withdraw.

Apex: The top of a shell in a snail, limpet or other gastropod.

Beak: The projecting part of the hinge in a bivalve.

Byssus (or Byssal threads): Tough silk-like threads secreted by a gland in the foot of some bivalves to anchor the valves to a solid substrate.

Callus: A tongue-like covering of the umbilicus.

Carapace: The hard covering or exoskeleton that covers the upper portion of a shrimp or crab.

Ceras (plural Cerata): The elongated projections on the back of an aeolid nudibranch, used in gas exchange as well as extensions of the digestive gland.

Cilia: Minute hair-like structures used for locomotion, food gathering and other functions.

Cirrus (plural Cirri): The modified legs of barnacles; soft hair-like or finger-like projections.

Ctenes: The comb plates of comb jellies.

Chondrophore: A spoon-shaped projection near the hinge on one shell of a bivalve.

Detritus: Debris that contains organic particles.

Dorid: A type of nudibranch that has a plume-like gill on its back.

Exoskeleton: An external skeleton, such as the shell of a crab.

Filter feeder: An organism that strains particles of food from the water.

Girdle: The muscular tissue that surrounds the eight valves of a chiton.

Nematocyst: A cell that releases a stinging thread, used for protection by jellies, sea anemones and related organisms.

Operculum: The calcareous or horn-like "trap door" that covers a snail for protection when it has retreated inside its shell.

Osculum (plural Oscula): The large excurrent pore through which water exits from a sponge.

Ostium: An incurrent pore through which water enters a sponge.

Parapodia: The lateral extensions on the side of each segment of segmented worms.

Pedicellariae: Pincer-like appendages found on sea stars and sea urchins.

Pelagic: Free-swimming in the ocean.

Polychaete: Segmented worms that have paddle-like appendages, well-developed sense organs, and many setae (hairs).

Polyp: An elongated individual organism (in the phylum Cnidaria) with a mouth that is surrounded by tentacles at one end and attached to a substrate at the other end.

Radula: A toothed, tongue-like ribbon in the mouth of a gastropod, used to rasp food from a hard surface.

Rhinophore: A large pair of antennae-like sensory organs found on the head of a nudibranch.

Spicule: A lime or glass rod that provides support for a sponge.

Test: The round internal skeleton of a sea urchin or sand dollar.

Umbilicus: The navel-like opening in the center of the columella (column-like structure), at the base of a true snail.

Umbo (or Umbone): The "beak" or prominent portion of the hinge on a bivalve.

Valve: Shell. One of 2 calcareous coverings of a bivalve. Also, one of the 8 shells of a chiton.

Veliger: A free-swimming larval mollusc with wing-like appendages.

Checklist of Seashore Creatures

SPONGES
- [ ] Bread Crumb Sponge
- [ ] Red Encrusting Sponge
- [ ] Purple Encrusting Sponge

ANEMONES, HYDROIDS & ALLIES
- [ ] Aggregating Anemone
- [ ] Giant Green Anemone
- [ ] Moonglow Anemone
- [ ] Short Plumose Anemone
- [ ] Painted Anemone
- [ ] Stubby Rose Anemone
- [ ] White-spotted Anemone
- [ ] Wine-glass Hydroid
- [ ] Turgid Garland Hydroid
- [ ] Ostrich-plume Hydroid
- [ ] Purple Encrusting Hydrocoral
- [ ] Solitary Pink-mouth Hydroid
- [ ] By-the-wind Sailor
- [ ] Cross Jelly
- [ ] Water Jelly
- [ ] Aggregating Jelly
- [ ] Lion's Mane Jelly
- [ ] Pacific Moon Jelly

MARINE WORMS
- [ ] Northern Feather-duster Worm
- [ ] Pile Worm
- [ ] Eighteen-paired Scaleworm

MOSS ANIMALS
- [ ] Kelp Encrusting Bryozoan
- [ ] Orange Encrusting Bryozoan
- [ ] Derby Hat Bryozoan

MOLLUSCS
- [ ] Lined Chiton
- [ ] Mossy Chiton
- [ ] Black Katy Chiton
- [ ] Giant Pacific Chiton
- [ ] Rough Keyhole Limpet
- [ ] Two-spot Keyhole Limpet
- [ ] Whitecap Limpet
- [ ] Ribbed Limpet
- [ ] Mask Limpet
- [ ] Pacific Plate Limpet
- [ ] Shield Limpet
- [ ] Fenestrate Limpet
- [ ] Checkered Periwinkle
- [ ] Sitka Periwinkle
- [ ] Blue Topsnail
- [ ] Black Turban
- [ ] Dusky Turban
- [ ] Frilled Dogwinkle
- [ ] Northern Striped Dogwinkle
- [ ] Channelled Dogwinkle
- [ ] Leafy Hornmouth
- [ ] Dire Whelk
- [ ] Purple Olive
- [ ] Lewis's Moonsnail
- [ ] Wrinkled Amphissa
- [ ] Mudflat Snail
- [ ] Red Nudibranch
- [ ] Monterey Dorid
- [ ] Sea Lemon
- [ ] Barnacle-eating Dorid
- [ ] Rufus Tipped Nudibranch
- [ ] Opalescent Nudibranch
- [ ] Ringed Nudibranch
- [ ] Shag-rug Nudibranch
- [ ] Frosted Nudibranch
- [ ] California Mussel
- [ ] Pacific Blue Mussel
- [ ] Northern Horsemussel
- [ ] Pacific Oyster
- [ ] Olympia Oyster
- [ ] Smooth Pink Scallop
- [ ] Spiny Pink Scallop
- [ ] Giant Rock Scallop
- [ ] Baltic Macoma
- [ ] Bent-nose Macoma
- [ ] White-sand Macoma
- [ ] Fat Gaper
- [ ] Pacific Gaper
- [ ] Nuttall's Cockle
- [ ] Purple Mahogany-clam

- [ ] California Sunset Clam
- [ ] Softshell-clam
- [ ] Pacific Razor-clam
- [ ] Pacific Littleneck
- [ ] Japanese Littleneck
- [ ] Butter Clam
- [ ] Flat-tip Piddock
- [ ] Rough Piddock
- [ ] Boring Softshell-clam

ARTHROPODS
- [ ] Thatched Barnacle
- [ ] Acorn Barnacle
- [ ] Goose Barnacle
- [ ] Pink Beach Hopper
- [ ] Sea Slater
- [ ] Monterey Isopod
- [ ] Vosnesensky's Isopod
- [ ] California Beach Hopper
- [ ] Blue Beach Hopper
- [ ] Skeleton Shrimp
- [ ] Stout Shrimp
- [ ] Smooth Bay Shrimp
- [ ] Bay Ghost Shrimp
- [ ] Blue Mud Shrimp
- [ ] Grainyhand Hermit
- [ ] Greenmark Hermit
- [ ] Hairy Hermit
- [ ] Blueband Hermit
- [ ] Red Rock Crab
- [ ] Dungeness Crab
- [ ] Flattop Crab
- [ ] Flat Porcelain Crab
- [ ] Shield-backed Kelp Crab
- [ ] European Green Crab
- [ ] Green Shore Crab
- [ ] Purple Shore Crab

SPINY-SKINNED ANIMALS
- [ ] Mottled Star
- [ ] Purple Star
- [ ] Pacific Blood Star
- [ ] Leather Star
- [ ] Bat Star
- [ ] Delicate Six-rayed Star
- [ ] Morning Sun Star
- [ ] Striped Sun Star

- [ ] Sunflower Star
- [ ] Dwarf Brittle Star
- [ ] Daisy Brittle Star
- [ ] Long-armed Brittle Star
- [ ] Black and White Brittle Star
- [ ] Eccentric Sand Dollar
- [ ] Green Sea Urchin
- [ ] Purple Sea Urchin
- [ ] Red Sea Urchin
- [ ] California Sea Cucumber
- [ ] Orange Sea Cucumber
- [ ] Stiff-footed Sea Cucumber

TUNICATES
- [ ] Spiny-headed Sea Squirt
- [ ] Stalked Sea Squirt
- [ ] Shiny Red Sea Squirt
- [ ] Taylor's Social Tunicate
- [ ] Lightbulb Tunicate
- [ ] Red Sea Pork
- [ ] California Sea Pork
- [ ] Mushroom Tunicate
- [ ] Harbour Star Ascidian

FISHES
- [ ] Tidepool Sculpin
- [ ] Plainfin Midshipman
- [ ] Northern Clingfish
- [ ] Crescent Gunnel

ADDITIONAL NOTES:

_____
_____
_____
_____
_____
_____
_____
_____
_____
_____
_____
_____

NOTE:
Additional checklists may be
found at www.septphoto.com

Index

About the Author

Duane Sept is a biologist, freelance writer and professional photographer. His biological work has included research on various wildlife species and service as a park naturalist. His award-winning photographs have been published internationally, in displays and in books, magazines and other publications, for clients that include BBC Wildlife, Parks Canada, Nature Canada, National Wildlife Federation and World Wildlife Fund.

Today Duane brings a wealth of information to the public as an author, in much the same way he has inspired thousands of visitors to Canada's parks. His published books include *The Beachcomber's Guide to Seashore Life in the Pacific Northwest* (Harbour Publishing) *The Beachcomber's Guide to Seashore Life of California* (Harbour Publishing) and *A Photographic Guide to the Seashore Life in the North Atlantic: Canada to Cape Cod* (Princeton University Press).

More Great Books from Calypso Publishing

Common Birds of British Columbia
J. Duane Sept

This full-color photographic guide features 136 species of birds found in British Columbia. Discover interesting facts about each species as well as descriptions, habitat and range. Handy tips are also included on how to bring birds closer, outfit yourself with birding equipment and attract birds to your backyard.

5.5" x 8.5" • 96 pages • 158 color photos • Softcover • $12.95 • ISBN 978-0-9739819-1-9

•••••••••••••••••••••••••••

Wild Berries of the Northwest:
Alaska, Western Canada and the Northwestern United States
J. Duane Sept

Fruits and berries are all around us. Identify these fruits and their flowers on your next trip to the ocean, lake or woods with this full-color guide. Learn which species are edible and which are poisonous. An entire chapter of mouth-watering recipes is also featured. Enjoy!

5.5" x 8.5" • 96 pages • 169 color photos • Softcover • $12.95 • ISBN 0-9730390-8-6

•••••••••••••••••••••••••••

Common Mushrooms of the Northwest:
Alaska, Western Canada and the Northwestern United States
J. Duane Sept

This full-color photographic guide features 130 species of mushrooms and other fungi found in the Northwest, from Alaska to Oregon—some edible, some poisonous, all intriguing. Besides a description of each species, the book includes habitat, range, edibility, tips on distinguishing similar species and other interesting information. There are also pointers on storing edible mushrooms, making spore prints and much more.

5.5" x 8.5" • 96 pages • 150 color photos • Softcover • $14.95 • ISBN 978-0-9739819-0-2

These titles are available at your local bookstore or

Calypso Publishing

www.calypso-publishing.com